Shropshire

In an age where over-development and noise are increasingly the norm, Shropshire remains, in the words of its famous poet A.E. Housman, one of 'the quietest places under the sun'. Despite its proximity to the industrial heartland of the West Midlands and its links with Ironbridge Gorge

history, it is largely untouched by 20th-century industry or major roads, and the patchwork fields of its rolling countryside hark back to the days when all cultivation was on a human scale.

Quietude should not be confused with somnolence however. Shropshire may be a county without a city but Shrewsbury, Ludlow and Bridgnorth are thriving historic and cultural towns with outstanding black-and-white architecture; Ironbridge Gorge is England's finest industrial heritage complex; and small market towns such as Much Wenlock, Bishop's Castle, Market Drayton and Oswestry also have much to offer. The remains of ancient fortifications and abbeys abound in town and countryside, while the great landmark of Offa's Dyke divides Shropshire from neighbouring Wales. For many more visitors these are all mere interludes to the county's glorious 'blue remembered hills', where walking offers the perfect blend of scenery, exercise and relaxation.

Sheep grazing on the Long Mynd.

SHREWSBURY

Black-and-white houses, Britain in Bloom and Brother Cadfael

'*High the Vanes of Shrewsbury gleam, Islanded in Severn Stream*', wrote A.E. Housman, describing the town's unique protected position, enclosed within a horseshoe loop of the meandering river.

•

Rowley's House, built in the 1590s, now houses the town's excellent history museum.

In medieval times, as now, the only way to reach the centre was to cross one of its bridges or the narrow neck of land guarded by its castle. Thanks to this site Shrewsbury grew as a stronghold, and in medieval times was used both to attack and to defend against the rebellious Welsh Princes of the borderlands. Meanwhile the town continued to prosper from the trade in Welsh wool. Its legacy is a host of magnificent black-and-white timber mansions built by the wool barons, which have earned Shrewsbury the title of 'England's finest Tudor town'. Don't miss Bear Steps Hall (in the charming precinct of St Alkmund's Church), Ireland's Mansion and Owen's Mansion (both on High Street), or Rowley's House (on Barker Street).

Wool, a valuable commodity in medieval times, entered Shrewsbury by the Welsh Bridge, was processed by the Drapers (wool merchants), and departed by the English Bridge (right).

Shrewsbury is linked with many famous historical personalities, including Charles Darwin (1809–82), who was born here and attended the famous Shrewsbury School, and Clive of India (1725–74) who was mayor and MP for the town. Darwin's statue sits opposite the castle, while the Clive House Museum is housed in the former home of Lord Clive during his term as mayor. The town's most famous fictional son is

Out and About

Acton Burnell Castle: Atmospheric 13th-century manor house ruins (English Heritage).
Attingham Park: An elegant 18th-century neo-classical mansion (National Trust).
Battlefield Church: Site of the Battle of Shrewbury (1403) between Henry Percy (Hotspur) and Henry IV. (Open Sunday afternoon only.)
Haughmond Abbey: Extensive peaceful 12th-century Abbey ruins (English Heritage).
Wroxeter: Vestiges of the Roman city of Vironium (English Heritage).

The Shrewsbury Quest, opposite the Abbey, brings to life the age of Brother Cadfael and sets visitors in the footsteps of the detective-monk.

DATE FOR THE DIARY
Shrewsbury Flower Show: August.

Brother Cadfael, of Shrewsbury Abbey, created by Shropshire lass Edith Pargeter (1913–95), who wrote under the pseudonym Ellis Peters.

The Abbey today is but a pale shadow of the powerful institution built by William the Conqueror's lieutenant, Roger de Montgomery, and where Cadfael was herbalist in the 12th century. Nonetheless it is still well worth a visit.

Shrewsbury is not just a black-and white town. In summer its buildings and streets are festooned in flowers and it has twice won the Britain in Bloom award. The Shrewsbury Flower Show is a major annual event and takes place around the Dingle, the beautiful formal flower gardens at the centre of the 29-acre Quarry riverside park.

Shrewsbury Castle: by the 14th century border hostilities had ceased and the castle was converted to a gaol, shire hall and then a private residence. Today it houses the Shropshire Regimental Museum.

IRONBRIDGE

The valley where the Industrial Revolution was forged

During the late-18th century, Ironbridge Gorge was lined with forges and furnaces, which lit up the sky day and night, causing a cacophony of noise, smog and pollution on an unthinkable scale.

•

Standing in the peaceful Ironbridge Gorge today it is almost impossible to believe that 250 years ago this area (then known as Coalbrookdale) was the most industrialised place on earth.

It all started in 1708–9 when Abraham Darby I came to this gorge which nature had blessed with coal, limestone, iron ore, timber and a navigable waterway. Darby's great achievement was to pioneer a cheap method of smelting iron (by using coke instead of expensive charcoal) and under his dynasty Coalbrookdale became not only the most important iron-producing area in the world, but the epicentre of the Industrial Revolution.

The Iron Bridge, cast and erected across the gorge in 1779, was both functional and a status symbol, remarkably constructed using woodworking techniques, as no other bridge technology was then available. Alongside the industrial might of the gorge, artistic endeavour also flourished. The famous

Coalport China Company started here, and across the river in Jackfield two of the world's largest ceramic tile companies created pieces of the highest quality.

By the early 20th century, however, Coalbrookdale's golden age was over. Nature began reclaiming the gorge and

Bedlam Furnaces: in 1787 Charles Dibdin wrote 'Coalbrookdale wants nothing but Cerberus to give you an idea of hell. The Severn may pass for the Styx'.

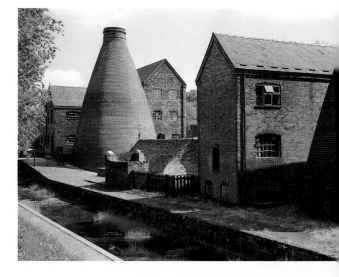

ackfield Tile Museum.

Telford

The new town of Telford, designated in 1965, was named after the great Scottish engineer, Thomas Telford (1757–1834), the first surveyor of the county of Shropshire. Today it is a thriving business and shopping centre. The main visitor attraction is the 250-acre Town Park which includes Wonderland, a themed area for small children.

by the 1950s most of its buildings had lapsed into dereliction.

Today the principal sites have been restored and give a fascinating insight into the great 'iron age'. The highlights are the Museum of Iron, describing the methods and achievements of the Darbys and their forgemasters; the original Iron Bridge toll-house, which tells the colourful story of this unique structure; the Coalport China Museum and the Jackfield Tile Museum (see above); and the Blists Hill Open Air Museum. The latter is a splendid re-creation of the small turn-of-the-century Coalbrookdale community of Blists Hill, peopled by costumed actors who demonstrate various aspects of their domestic and working lives including trades, crafts, and industrial techniques.

Visitors came from all over the world to marvel at 'a Fabric which England or the whole Global cannot equal', and its name passed to the small town that grew up around it.

5

ABOVE THE SEVERN

at Bridgnorth

Bridgnorth is a charming black-and-white market town, with a split personality. Low Town, in the now sylvan valley of the Severn, was once the river port; High Town, perched on the red sandstone cliff 200ft above, is the historic centre of Bridgnorth.

●

Low Town and High Town are connected by a vertiginous funicular railway, dating from 1892, and seven steep stairways. The most rewarding of these is Cartway, containing cave dwellings which were inhabited as recently as 1856, and the splendid black-and-white Bishop Percy's House, built in 1580.

The bustling High Street features several fine 17th-century buildings including the Town Hall, perched on a sandstone arched base; The Swan, an old coaching inn; and the North Gate, the only surviving gate from the original fortifications.

Out and About

Dudmaston: A late 17th-century house with fine furnishings including modern art and sculptures (National Trust).

Midland Motor Museum: Over 100 sports and racing vehicles dating back to the 1920s.

Just off the top of the High Street, at the highest point of the town, is St Leonard's Church. Around it is a close with more outstanding 17th-century buildings – Palmer's Hospital alms-houses, the Grammar School, and Richard Baxter's House.

At the bottom end of the High Street are the imposing Italianate New Market Buildings, now home to craft galleries and the Museum of Costume and Childhood.

From Castle Walk there is a magnificent panorama over the Severn and surrounding hills. The castle, behind, was destroyed by Cromwell's forces – along with much of the centre of Bridgnorth – in 1645. Only a huge section of the keep still stands, leaning precariously at a crazy angle of 15° (around three times the incline of Pisa's famous tower!).

St Leonard's Church, glimpsed from the High Street.

The castle grounds also look down onto the Severn Valley Railway station. This is the northern end of a popular privately operated line which follows the river through 16 miles of beautiful wooded countryside, terminating south at Kidderminster. Just south of Bridgnorth it passes on a 19th-century viaduct almost right overhead Daniel's Mill. This is an idyllically located, beautifully restored corn mill open to the public.

In 1642 Charles I stayed at Bridgnorth Castle for three days and called the view from Castle Walk 'the fairest in the dominion'.

The Severn Valley Railway Company boasts the largest working steam collection in Britain.

LUDLOW

Shropshire's historic gem

A strong contender for the title of 'England's finest small town', Ludlow enjoys a splendid position high above the river Teme. It is famous for its castle, its wide streets full of historic houses (500 of which are listed) and a parish church of cathedral-like grandeur.

•

It was the Normans who built the town's massive castle in 1085 to tame the Marches and in the 14th century it was expanded into a palace fit for royalty. Although partially destroyed after the English Civil War, much of its structure still remains intact.

Near the castle entrance Ludlow's history can be traced in the town museum and at the Old Castle Lodge, now open to the public as an historic house.

The spacious market place has thrived since medieval times when the town was a great wool centre, and the riches of this period made possible the foundation of the imposing 15th-century Church of St Laurence. It is one of the largest parish churches in England, with many impressive fittings and monuments. Climb its tower for magnificent views ranging south to Titterstone Clee Hill (1749ft) and north to Brown Clee Hill (1772ft), the highest point in Shropshire.

Many of Ludlow's finest structures lie on Broad Street, a most handsome

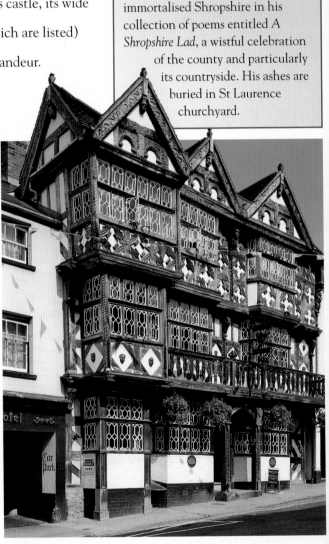

A Shropshire Lad

A.E. Housman (1859–1936) immortalised Shropshire in his collection of poems entitled A Shropshire Lad, a wistful celebration of the county and particularly its countryside. His ashes are buried in St Laurence churchyard.

The Feathers Hotel, praised by the architectural historian Pevsner as 'that prodigy of timber-framed houses'.

Mighty Ludlow Castle, where Catherine of Aragon and Mary Tudor were entertained, and the ill-fated 'Little Princes' detained.

thoroughfare which climbs steeply from the 15th-century Ludford Bridge to the 18th-century Buttercross. Its buildings span the same age from half-timbered to elegant Georgian dwellings, a reminder that the town was a fashionable social centre during the 18th and 19th centuries. Most admired of all Ludlow's buildings is The Feathers Hotel, a 17th-century inn with a lavish façade. Opposite, The Bull Hotel is thought to be the town's oldest inn, dating from the 15th century.

Cleobury Mortimer, 12 miles east of Ludlow, is an attractive village with a landmark crooked church spire. William Langland (c.1332–c.1400), the author of the famous early English poem *Piers Plowman* (c.1362), may have been born in the village, and a church window is dedicated to him.

The classic view of Ludlow – from Whitcliffe Common.

DATES FOR THE DIARY
Ludlow Festival: An internationally acclaimed arts festival, featuring an open-air Shakespeare play in the castle grounds: late June/early July.
Summer Sundays: Events and special markets in the market square.

SHROPSHIRE HILLS

and a Long Mountain

The Long Mynd (*mynd/mynydd* is Welsh for mountain) is both figuratively and literally the centrepiece of South Shropshire. It comprises 4–5 sq miles of wild moorland plateau, its higher slopes covered with gorse and bracken and its eastern side intersected by many steep valleys. Much of the Mynd is owned by the National Trust (NT).

•

This is the finest walking territory in the county and the favourite starting point is the Carding Mill Valley, just outside Church Stretton, where there is a NT information centre and café. Topographical models, walking trails (for all levels of ability) and NT ranger-guided walks set visitors on their way.

An ancient track known as The Port Way runs right along the crest of the Long Mynd for some eight miles. In prehistoric times this was used by drovers and axe traders and there are several earthen barrows to either side of the track. A narrow road, accessible by car, follows the ridge but beware if driving anywhere on the Long Mynd, as the roads can be very narrow and in summer congestion is likely.

Despite its appearance, Little Stretton Church only dates back to the 1920s.

On the opposite side of the A49 from the Long Mynd lie the Stretton Hills, an old volcanic range with three notable peaks, Ragleth Hill (1247ft), The Lawley (1236ft) and Caer Caradoc (1506ft), all providing splendid views over the countryside below. Caer Caradoc (the Hill of Caractacus) is claimed to be the site where the legendary British chieftain Caractacus was finally defeated by the Romans in 50 AD. This theory is given some credence by the remains of an ancient British hill fort near the summit.

Church Stretton is a pleasant village which today mostly feeds and waters weary walkers, though in Victorian times it was a thriving health resort. Its fine church is part Norman, part 17th-century and is notable for its 13th-century roof and a fertility figure (over the north door) of Saxon origin. The adjacent village of Little Stretton also features a charming and unusual church, black-and-white timbered with a thatched roof. There is another valley approach to the Long Mynd at Little Stretton, known as Ashes Hollow, which is much less frequented than the Carding Mill Valley but still very attractive.

Acton Scott Farm, just off the A49, re-creates farm life at the turn of the century in a beautiful setting. Daily demonstrations include milking by

Good old-fashioned baking demonstrated at Acton Scott Farm.

hand, butter-making and old-fashioned baking, while farriers, blacksmiths and wheelwrights pay weekly visits.

The Long Mynd from Caer Caradoc.

ALONG THE EDGE

Wenlock Edge

Wenlock Edge is a narrow wooded limestone escarpment, running diagonally north-east to south-west, from just north of Much Wenlock to Craven Arms. Strange as it may seem today, Wenlock Edge was once a coral reef, formed when Britain lay on the equator, and it is still famous for its unusual flora. Most of the Edge is owned by the National Trust who provide car parking and walking trails.

The rolling greenery of Wenlock Edge.

●

Wenlock Edge escarpment rises between 800 and 950ft above sea level, offering panoramic views west (particularly from the Ippikins Rock, near the Wenlock Edge Inn) with Shropshire's classic patchwork countryside spreading out below as far as the Stiperstones and the Wrekin. In the foreground lies the pretty village of Hughley, which features in *A Shropshire Lad* (see page 8).

Much Wenlock is one of the most delightful small towns in the county, with a wealth of historic buildings, including a rare surviving town farm. It is most famous for the picturesque and extensive medieval ruins of Wenlock Priory, set in lovely gardens.

Look into the town's colourful small museum where you'll discover the fascinating history of the Much Wenlock Olympian Games, initiated in 1850 by a local doctor, William Penny Brookes (who also introduced physical education to British schools). The Games, which inspired the modern Olympic movement, are still held today.

Opposite is the splendid 16th-century Guildhall. This building also housed the medieval gaol and the whipping post is still evident below. The town council continues to sit upstairs and it is well worth a visit to see the magnificent woodwork in their chambers.

Just beyond the southern tip of Wenlock Edge lies Stokesay Castle, largely built between 1285 and 1305. The oldest part is the unique half-timbered storey atop the North Tower. Its battlements and moat indicate its defensive posture, though it never fired (or received) a shot in anger and thus preserved its fabric. Like Wenlock Priory, its colourful history is brought to life by a self-guided English Heritage audio tour.

The castle forms a beautiful grouping alongside a picturesque half-timbered yellow gatehouse, which dates from 1570 (with Jacobean trimmings) and an atmospheric church, mostly rebuilt in the 17th century but still retaining some Norman features.

DATES FOR THE DIARY
Much Wenlock Olympian Games:
mid July.

Wenlock Priory, the finest medieval ruins in the county.

Stokesay Castle, the oldest and most handsome fortified manor-house in England.

ON THE BORDER

Castles, earthworks and a rocky ridge

The Marches, or borderlands, are the western most fringe of Shropshire, featuring great swathes of rolling, remote, sparsely populated countryside. To the west is Wales, to the east is England, a frontier marked since the late 8th century by the earth bank known as Offa's Dyke.

Bishop's Castle Town Hall and Michaelmas celebration flags.

The most romantic of the Marches strongholds is Whittington Castle (three miles east of Oswestry), built in 1221. However, its powerful twin towers are a mere façade. Behind, little remains.

King Offa of Mercia was the architect of this 'Great Wall' which runs for 176 miles and is up to 25ft tall, often with a wide ditch on the Welsh side. It is presumed to be a defensive rampart and (taking into account 12 centuries of erosion) may originally have been up to 50ft tall. The Offa's Dyke Long Distance Path closely follows the ancient bank and there is an Offa's Dyke information centre at Knighton, just across the Welsh border.

Fortifications have always been a feature of the Marches and heading north is Clun, its once sturdy castle now in ruins. The town straddles the River Clun via a 16th-century bridge, and its town hall, once a gaol, now houses a museum.

There's no longer a castle at Bishop's Castle, but there is plenty of interest in this charming small town. A colourful local museum now occupies the 16th-century House on Crutches, the best of several well-preserved half-timbered buildings. And a little further up the hill, behind the picturesque black-and-white house that was formerly the Bull Inn, is a railway museum.

The Marches' most famous natural feature is the Stiperstones, a ridge topped by a three-mile-long outcrop of quartzite, now designated a National Nature Reserve. It is a great favourite with walkers, offering magnificent views from its peak of 1762ft. Lead and minerals have been quarried here for centuries, and the topography is harsher than elsewhere on the Shropshire Hills. Sinister legends abound, and the northern-most rock outcrop is known as

the Devil's Chair. Inevitably stories also attach to Mitchell's Fold, an ancient stone circle, some three miles due west.

The north-west corner of Shropshire holds more evidence of early man. The Old Oswestry Hill Fort is one of the largest and most elaborate earthworks of its kind, occupying an area of 68 acres. Oswestry itself is an attractive town with several historic buildings and a Transport Museum. Begin the tour at the Old Grammar School Heritage and Tourist Information Centre, housed in a beautiful 15th-century building.

One of the best-preserved stretches of Offa's Dyke is Spring Hill/Llanfair Hill, north of Knighton. At 1408ft, this is also the highest point of the Dyke, and offers views for miles around.

GARDENS AND WATERWAYS

of North Shropshire

The attractions of North Shropshire may not be immediately obvious; there are no famous towns, nor any major historical attractions. Yet almost hidden away in this less-visited part of the county are some outstanding parks and gardens, lovely lakes and picturesque stretches of the once-bustling Shropshire Union Canal.

•

Market Drayton is the chief town of the north renowned for its gingerbread and the antics of young Robert Clive of India, who seems to have spent much of his youth fighting other boys, terrorising local shopkeepers and scaling the tower of St Mary's Church. Close to the church is the Old Grammar School (now a private house) which he attended.

Market Drayton features some fine 17th-century architecture but the best local black-and-white building is Old Colehurst Manor, to the south. Recently restored, its new owners turn the clock back 400 years with period cooking and costume, for day visitors or overnight guests.

Close by at Hodnet are two very contrasting outdoor attractions. Like Old Colehurst Manor, Hawkstone Historic Park and Follies has also recently been rescued from dereliction and slumber and restored to its Victorian heyday when it was one of the wonders of northern England. Begun in the 18th century, it is a remarkable 400-acre scenic semi-natural park of lookout peaks on high sandstone outcrops, a grotto (where King Arthur 'himself' will

Crossing the Swiss Bridge at Hawkstone Historic Park.

Hodnet Hall Gardens, a riot of late spring and early summer colours, but a delight all year round with pools and woods.

The Mere, Ellesmere – at 116 acres mere only in name.

convince you that this was once his home) a cleft, tunnels, bridges, follies and historic models, all linked by hilly, often steep, pathways. It's a relatively strenuous trek but is well worth the effort. Visitors who wish to stay on a level plain in more formal surroundings will enjoy nearby Hodnet Hall Gardens and (to the north west, near Willough-bridge) the Dorothy Clive Garden.

South of Hodnet is Moreton Corbet Castle. Very little remains of the original medieval castle but the ruined shell of the adjacent grandiose Elizabethan mansion is very impressive.

The region around Ellesmere is known as Shropshire's Lake District, with some good-sized meres (lakes) and the Shropshire Union Canal passing right through the town. Ellesmere is a pleasant small market town where you can admire the gaily painted barges moored at the Wharf or take a rowing boat out on The Mere (the town's 116-acre lake). The two other main settlements of the area are Wem and Whitchurch, both quiet market towns featuring typically fine examples of black-and-white buildings.

> ### DATES FOR THE DIARY
> **Ellesmere Festival**, including a colourful procession of barges from all over the country: mid September.

EAST SHROPSHIRE

A royal oak, stately grandeur and heavenly pursuits

For many visitors the eastern approach (along the M54) is the gateway to Shropshire and their first significant sighting is the Wrekin, a ubiquitous and well-loved landmark. This great mound, once volcanic, bursts abruptly from the flat Shropshire Plain to a summit of 1334ft, where Iron Age tribes once sought the security of high ground and built their earthworks. Today on the Wrekin man builds television transmitters. The views from here are outstanding.

•

Before hurrying on to Ironbridge or Shrewsbury, exit at junction 3 of the motorway. Immediately north is the distinctive 15th-century church of St Bartholomew at Tong. Originally a Collegiate church, its numerous superb 16th-century monuments have led to the soubriquet of 'the village Westminster Abbey' and were also featured by Charles Dickens as a setting in *The Old Curiosity Shop*.

The famous Royal Oak is, alas, a mere descendant of the original – despite the claims of the attached Victorian plaque.

Three miles east is Boscobel House with authentic royal connections. It was here in 1651 (after the Battle of Worcester) that King Charles II was concealed to evade capture by Cromwell. He spent a night in a small hiding place in the house and a night in the famous 'royal oak' tree in the grounds. Boscobel House itself is a romantic 17th-century timber-framed hunting lodge, restored to re-create an atmospheric evocation of the period. Follow the country roads to Weston-under-Lizard and Weston Park. With

DATES FOR THE DIARY
RAF Open Day at Cosford, a flying spectacular normally including the Red Arrows: June.
Weston Park Classical Music Festival: mid August.
Weston Park Midland Game and Country Sports Fair: mid September.

sumptuous furnishings and tapestries, and paintings by Van Dyck, Holbein and Gainsborough, it is arguably the county's finest stately home. Its grounds feature a deer park and several family attractions, and are host to many popular events throughout the year.

Lilleshall Abbey, a few miles north west, is better known for its modern centre of sporting excellence than for its original Augustinian institution. Now ruined, the powerful west front is an impressive reminder of the former church and cloisters. Two miles north, Newport boasts an attractive high street featuring many architectural periods.

Back across the motorway, RAF Cosford is another famous sporting name, host to international athletics

meetings. On the same site is the Cosford Aerospace Museum, one of the largest collections of its kind in the country, with over 80 aircraft on permanent display, including warplanes from World War II to the present day; civil transport aircraft; research and development curiosities; missiles, rockets and aero engines.

A 1940s Hurricane MK11a at Cosford Aerospace Museum.

Weston Park, a handsome brick mansion built in 1671 and formerly the seat of the Earls of Bradford.

Walking in Shropshire

Up hills, down dales and along escarpments

Whatever your age, ability or inclinations, Shropshire is perfect walking country. As Murray's Travel Companion put it over a century ago, 'Salop (Shropshire) contains within the compass of a few miles all the characteristics of an Alpine District in miniature, while at the same time within sight of orchards, gardens and farmhouses'.

●

The county's favourite highland stamping grounds are the Long Mynd, the Stretton Hills, the Stiperstones, Wenlock Edge and the Clee Hills. From the urban surroundings of Shrewsbury and Telford New Town the Wrekin always beckons, while on the Marches the Offa's Dyke Long Distance Path and the wild Clun Forest are powerful attractions. However, almost anywhere in Shropshire is within easy reach of a good walk and hiking boots are rarely obligatory. Meander beside the Meres in the north, stroll by the Severn in the south, saunter along the Shropshire Union Canal towpath or tap into one of several long-distance paths that traverse the county; the Shropshire Way, the Marches Way, the Silkin Way, Wild Edric's Way, the Mortimer Trail. There is a wealth of information and literature on all these trails and on general walking in Shropshire in any tourist information centre.

Hiking on the south-west ridge of the Wrekin. In the distance, across the Vale of Severn, rise Caer Caradoc and the Long Mynd.